Soaring Century

100 Years of Langley Air Force Base

Langley Air Force Base

HAMPTON

64

64

664

VIRGINIA

Hampton

Soaring Century

100 Years of Langley
Air Force Base

By Mark St. John Erickson
with Hugh Lessig and Ryan Murphy

Edited by Jim Manner, David Hendrickson
and Shana Gray

Soaring Century
100 Years of Langley Air Force Base

Text copyright © 2016 by Daily Press Media Group

Editing by Jim Manner, David Hendrickson and Shana Gray
Design by Shana Gray
Cover design by Wayne Elfman

Daily Press Media Group
Marisa Porto, publisher and editor-in-chief
703 Mariners Row
Newport News, VA 23606
dailypress.com

Printed in the United States of America

Contents

Foreword 1

Introduction 3

Taking flight 5

Molding modern Hampton 17

Storied squadrons 25

Bombs away! 33

Leviathan's fiery end 45

B-17s blaze trail 55

Additional photos 65

Foreword

Congratulations Langley Air Force Base on 100 years of dedicated service to our community and nation!

We began our long association with LAFB when biplanes were still in the air, Franklin D. Roosevelt was president, and we were called Laboratory Federal Credit Union.

Together we have witnessed, and been a part of, tremendous cultural and technological change.

Throughout the years, Langley Federal Credit Union has been proud to have had an active role in meeting the needs of our Langley Air Force Base members whose hard work, dedication and sacrifice have done so much to keep our community strong and our nation safe.

Here's to another 100 years!

The Board, Staff and Members of Langley Federal Credit Union

The first plane at Langley Field was a Curtiss JN-4 "Jenny" biplane, which became operational in mid-1917 and for many years was the workhorse aircraft at the base. *Air Combat Command History Office photo*

Introduction

Virginia's Peninsula is packed with reminders of its role in military history. From Yorktown, to Fort Monroe, to the banks of the James River, the area is richly woven into the fate and formation of our nation.

Langley Air Force Base has been part of that historic fabric for 100 years. Throughout Langley's existence — as it transitioned from backwater swamp to a shining light of aviation and innovation — the Daily Press has covered every milestone.

We look forward to continuing that coverage for another century, and beyond.

The Daily Press is proud to present its look back at the first 100 years of Langley. We extend our congratulations to those who have passed through the Peninsula and lifted Langley's legacy.

Marisa Porto
Publisher and Editor-in-Chief, Daily Press Media Group

In this photo from June 11, 1921, S.E. 5a biplanes are shown during an aerial review and inspection at Langley Field. *Air Combat Command History Office photo*

4

Taking flight

By Mark St. John Erickson

Nearly 100 years after the first plane took off from Langley Field, it can be hard to see this busy stretch of land along Hampton's Back River as anything other than one of the most important hubs of American air power on the planet.

Lightning-fast F-22 Raptors from the 1st Fighter Wing carve up the skies overhead, patrolling the air with a stealthy, all-weather fighter unmatched by any foreign aircraft.

Air Combat Command works tirelessly in many of the buildings below, managing a vast legion of battle-ready Air Force units with a lethal global reach.

But when the first officers from the fledgling Aviation Section of the Army Signal Corps came to evaluate what is now Langley Air Force Base in late 1916, what they saw was not a highly developed complex of airplane hangars and runways but rather a backcountry expanse of fields, woods and old plantation homes.

Only in their imaginations could they envision the pioneering military aviation center that — despite almost closing following the turbulent days of World War I — would play an indispensable role in defining the potential of air power and the importance of a separate, wholly independent Air Force.

Few Army strategists of the day saw the promise of an invention still widely regarded as a novel reconnaissance tool rather than a combat weapon.

Lt. Col. George O. Squier was a champion of aeronautics. *Library of Congress photo*

So when Lt. Col. George Owen Squier and his selection board — including the Army's first rated pilot — recommended the 1,659-acre tract as the site of the service's first purpose-built air field, they were betting their futures on a revolutionary gamble.

"Aviation was still so new that there was a lot of resistance — even from the chief of the Signal Corps," Deputy Command Historian William M. Butler said.

"But Squier was very forward-thinking when it came to the airplane's potential. He saw them doing things that the planes of the day still couldn't do."

Driving force

An 1887 graduate of West Point, Squier was as much a scientist, engineer and inventor as a soldier.

So impressive was his grasp of mathematics, physics and ballistics that the Army sent him to Johns Hopkins University, where in 1893 he became the first officer to earn a Ph.D.

Following a tour of duty as an artillery instructor at Fort Monroe, Squier transferred to the Signal Corps, where he studied the emerging field of radio with pioneering Italian inventor Guglielmo Marconi.

"Squier was this rare combination of scholar, soldier and visionary," says aviation historian Amy Waters Yarsinske, author of "Flyboys Over Hampton Roads: Glenn Curtiss's Southern Experiment."

"That made him a powerhouse in the early history of military aviation."

After founding the Signal Corps School in 1905, Squier became a champion of aeronautics, spurring the creation of the Army's first aviation entity — the "Aeronautical Division" — in 1907.

A year later he completed a nationally influential paper on the military potential of aircraft — then bought the Corps' first airplane.

Soon Squier had allied with the Smithsonian Institution to propose a national advisory committee for aviation, historians Paul W. Clark and Lawrence A. Lyons note in their 2014 book "George Owen Squier: U.S. Army Major General, Inventor, Aviation Pioneer, Founder of Muzak."

He was still pressing Congress for support when World War I broke out in Europe, leading him to a secret mission and a firsthand look at the revolutionary military aviation innovations cropping up with breathtaking speed on the Western Front.

Returning in May 1916, Squier's report spurred approval for a "permanent experimental and inspection station" designed to help America catch up.

Such a place had never been built before, but it was "an absolute and immediate necessity for the proper and rapid development of Army aviation," he wrote.

"Squier was a moving force," Butler said, "a key figure in the Army's aviation aspirations at a time when the program was still very undefined and very small."

Mammoth deal

Exactly how some of Hampton's first citizens discovered the Army's plans may never be unraveled.

Among them was Clerk of Court Harry Holt Sr., who may have learned of the Signal Corps' search for a likely site from his powerful patron — U.S. Sen. Thomas S. Martin of Virginia — who chaired the Appropriations Committee.

Another leader was merchant Hunter R. Booker, whose niece had married an officer on the Corps' selection committee, known as the Aerodrome Board.

The gregarious Holt may have known Squier previously, too, because of the frequent dinner invitations he extended to officers at Fort Monroe, his grandson Wythe Holt Jr. recalls.

GENERAL PLAN LANGLEY FIELD
HAMPTON VIRGINIA

Architect Albert Kahn's plan called for a landing field, hangars, offices and living quarters stretching to the east from the King Street traffic circle along the Back River. His original timeline for completion was three to four years. *Air Combat Command History Office photo*

Then there's the link with the Curtiss Flying School in nearby Newport News, where aviation pioneer Glenn Curtiss and his manager — famed balloonist Thomas Baldwin — were not only exploring property near Hampton to expand but also past instructors at the Corps' aviation school.

Another possible source is Maj. William "Billy" Mitchell — a former Signal Corps instructor and a member of Squier's Washington, D.C., staff.

Every weekend during the fall of 1916 he traveled to the Curtiss School in order to take flying lessons and earn his pilot's license.

He also went gunning for ducks on the local rivers, the Daily Press reported.

"This was a very tight group. They all gravitated to each other and knew each other's business — and they knew this was the place to be," Yarsinske said, citing Curtiss' previous choice of Newport News and his participation in the Army's visits to the Back River.

"The climate was great for flying. It was in the middle of the East Coast. It was right on the water. It was close to Washington. It had everything they needed and wanted."

8

Still, spurred by worries over Virginia's looming prohibition law and its impact on the Old Point Comfort resort business, the Hampton men sweetened what became an irresistible offer.

In addition to obtaining options on more than 1,650 acres of relatively flat waterfront land, they secured the right of way to build a bridge and a streetcar line from Hampton.

They also promised electricity and water.

Though the property appears to have been favored from the start, the Army inspected it several times, including a Nov. 18 visit in which Squier brought the secretary of the Navy, the head of the Smithsonian and other members of the newly formed National Advisory Committee for Aeronautics, who had agreed to share the site.

"Mammoth Army aviation school and experimental station will be located on Back River near Hampton," the Dec. 17, 1916, Daily Press reported after the $290,000 deal was announced.

"The people of Hampton, Phoebus and Elizabeth City County have been given a wonderful Christmas gift."

Visionary plan

Even before the contract was signed on Dec. 30, 1916, Squier and his partners at NACA, which later became NASA, had big ideas for the new complex.

"This was going to be the first place built expressly as a military airfield — and they wanted to make a statement," retired Air Force historian Edward G. Longacre says.

"They wanted it to be the end-all and be-all of military bases. They wanted it to be a place like no other."

Traveling to Squier's home state of Michigan in November, the group met with automobile magnate Henry Ford, who recommended Albert Kahn of Detroit as the architect.

As seen in such landmark industrial structures as the 1903 Packard Motor Car plant and the giant Ford assembly plant started in Highland Park in 1909, Kahn had made a name for himself by taking on commissions for buildings that were the first of their kind.

So he seemed like the perfect choice for the groundbreaking avia-

Capt. John O. Steger of the Army Quartermaster Corps opened Langley Field's first official offices on the third floor of the Bank of Hampton on Feb. 2, 1917, while architect Albert Kahn began sketching the complex. *Air Force Historical Research Agency photo*

tion station that — as early as in a Dec. 17 editorial in the Daily Press — already was being referred to as the namesake of the late Smithsonian president and flight pioneer Samuel P. Langley.

"This was the sort of thing Kahn had cut his teeth on," said University of Michigan architectural historian Claire Zimmerman.

"From the master plan to the smallest details, he did these sorts of unprecedented projects really well."

Setting to work in February 1917 — the same month the Army opened Langley's first offices in a downtown Hampton bank building — Kahn and his staff quickly confirmed their reputations, sketching out ideas for an innovative complex that was part college campus and aeronautical village, as well as a model airfield.

But in addition to laying out the master plan, buildings and roads,

10

This detail of the Army Laboratory Building, completed in mid-1919, shows the decorative brickwork and aviation icon that distinguished Albert Kahn's designs for Langley Field. *Air Combat Command History Office photo*

CHANGING FIGHTERS

Clockwise from top, the F-22 Raptor, F-86 Sabre, F-15 Eagle and the A-10/OA-10 Thunderbolt II fly during a heritage flight during the Air Power over Hampton Roads air show at Langley Air Force Base in 2007. *Daily Press file photo*

they went far beyond the utilitarian requirements of the project, paying close attention to how the structures articulated their founders' ambitions for aviation's future.

Decorative brickwork and iconographical emblems abounded, including such tell-tale touches as the shields, stars, propellers, gears, winged eagles and pilots' badges that embellished the most prominent facades and entryways.

But even such inconspicuous features as the manhole covers — which bore the crossed-flag insignia of the Signal Corps — were recruited as heralds of Langley's higher purpose.

"Squier gave Kahn carte blanche — and he threw his whole heart and soul into the project," Longacre says.

"You have to marvel at how much work he put into these grandiose buildings. But everything changed when the war started."

Thwarted goals

Two months after Kahn began, the United States entered World War I, creating an immediate clash between the urgency of the

Despite its recent strong association with fighter planes — including the F-15 Eagle and F-22 Raptor that have dominated the skies over the field since 1976 — Langley Air Force Base didn't get its own operational fighter unit until April 1, 1931.

That's when the 8th Pursuit Group arrived, according to Air Force historians in "Langley Field: The Early Years 1916-1946," and with them came a series of more than a half-dozen pursuit — or fighter — planes that were constantly changing.

Made up of the 33rd, 35th, 36th and 37th squadrons, the airmen began training in such early aircraft as the Curtiss P-6 Hawk, a fast and maneuverable biplane with a top speed of more than 200 mph and a range of 285 miles.

By the late 1930s, they were flying the Curtiss P-36 Hawk, a single-wing fighter with a top speed of 313 mph and a range of 625 miles.

They also helped test the Curtiss YP-37, a prototype that — along with the P-36 — led to the development of the famous Curtiss P-40 Warhawk used by the Flying Tigers in China during World War II.

Mark St. John Erickson

war effort and his design and construction timeline of three to four years.

Even before then, the project had bogged down because of the unexpected difficulty of clearing, filling and grading the mostly wooded, low-lying site.

"Look at the photos of the surveyors. Look at their feet," says John V. Quarstein, author of "World War I on the Virginia Peninsula."

"Two guys have waders on. The others have tall boots. And all of them are covered with mud."

So demanding was the job of remaking the land that, over the course of a year, the Atlantic, Gulf and Pacific Co. deposited 1.8 million cubic meters of fill dredged from the Back River at a cost of $500,000, writes James R. Hansen in "Engineer in Charge: A History of the Langley Aeronautical Laboratory."

But the water table was still so high and land so susceptible to flooding during heavy rain and high tides that J.G. White Engineering Corp. had to construct a subsoil drainage system using ceramic

13

tiles.

"Nature's greatest ambition was to produce in this, her cesspool, the muddiest mud, the weediest weeds, the dustiest dust and the most ferocious mosquitoes the world has ever known," wrote one of the first soldiers assigned to the field.

"Her plans were so well formulated and adhered to that she far surpassed her wildest hopes and desires."

Wartime labor and material shortages slowed the work still more, Longacre says, forcing the Army to begin erecting temporary corrugated-metal aircraft hangars and tar paper barracks while waiting for Kahn to finish designing the permanent structures.

The officers in charge brought in prefabricated bungalows as a stopgap measure, too, providing the growing number of soldiers with not only housing but also offices and storage.

Adding to the confusion was the arrival of scores of British, French and Italian airmen, as well as boatloads of Allied planes sent to Langley for testing.

Then there was the mounting friction between the contractor and the Quartermaster Corps' superintendent of construction — who also clashed continuously with the field's commander.

By late fall, Squier was ready to write Langley off as "the bottleneck of the aircraft program."

That's when the Army moved its experimental aviation mission to McCook Field in Ohio, which already had installed the dynamometer needed to test the new Liberty engine.

"That should have been one of the first things Langley did," Longacre says.

"But due to the war they were trying to make the field operational at the same time they were building it.

"It was chaos."

New mission

Though stripped of one of its primary reasons for being, Langley served throughout the war as one of the principal fields for evaluating both foreign and domestic planes.

So numerous were the flights of British de Havillands, French

Nieuports and Italian Capronis over Hampton that the Daily Press regularly covered the exploits of the "foreign colony," who vied to set the latest speed, endurance and altitude records.

"The Europeans were far more advanced than us when it came to aircraft," Yarsinske said.

"We brought them here to teach us."

The pressing need for aerial reconnaissance filled Langley's hangars and barracks, too, after the School of Aerial Photography opened in October 1917.

By January it had sent its first graduates to the front, and it continued to oversee the final stages of training after the bulk of instruction moved to the Eastman Kodak Co. in New York.

Still, after spending more than $4 million, Langley had only one complete permanent structure.

And though two others were finished by the war's end on Nov. 11, 1918, the Army seemed ready to retrench.

"Everything was half-finished. It was a mess," Longacre said.

"And it looked like it all was going to come to a stop."

With hundreds of wartime bases being shuttered, Langley nearly closed, too.

But by early 1919, the stop-work order had been lifted — and the Army was spending nearly $1 million to finish what it had started.

Many factors contributed to this new lease on life, including new peacetime missions housing lighter-than-air dirigibles as well as aerial coastal defense and observation units linked closely to the artillery command at Fort Monroe.

The bombing range at nearby Plumtree Island also gave the newly arrived 2nd Bombardment Group a vast and virtually unrestricted place in which to conduct training that would later prove historic.

"In the end, Langley not only survived but grew," Butler said.

"And that's because the things that made it so attractive in the first place still applied."

The King Street gate to Langley is shown in this undated photo. The arrival of Langley changed many things in the area, including transportation, industry, culture and landscape. *Air Combat Command History Office photo*

Molding modern Hampton

By Ryan Murphy

Every aspect of daily life in Elizabeth City County changed after the arrival of the planes and airships at what is now known as Langley Air Force Base.

The city of Hampton, as Elizabeth City County is now known, would look like a very different place if not for the influence of the military installation that started as a modest testing field for propeller-driven planes and eventually played a critical role in getting Americans into space and to the moon.

Industry, transportation, culture, the landscape and even the dating scene took a dramatic turn in the decades that followed the birth of Langley Field, which celebrated its centennial in 2016.

"At the turn of the century, Hampton was a prosperous center of the seafood world, and it was pastoral. You had farms surrounding the town," said Mike Cobb, former curator of the Hampton History Museum.

"There were five or six major antebellum plantations where Langley is today — large farms," Cobb said. "Almost overnight, pastures

17

Early airships fly over what was later known as Langley's lighter-than-air area in this undated photo. *First Fighter Wing History Office photo*

are transformed into fields of flight and space exploration. Where once there were barns, now there were huge facilities for aircraft," such as the hangar for the massive airship Roma.

Langley Field, then a test site for the newly conceived U.S. Army Air Corps, began organizing in the north end of Elizabeth City County in December 1916. NASA's predecessor, the National Advisory Committee for Aeronautics, broke ground on its first laboratory there seven months later.

A changing landscape

John V. Quarstein, a Hampton Roads historian and author, said what started as a landing strip and a handful of propeller-driven planes would change the face and the soul of Elizabeth City County forever.

"It was a big deal in every matter. Langley changed the landscape for the city of Hampton and, in many ways, prompted it to become a city and not just a town in a county," Quarstein said.

Villages at Buckroe, Fox Hill and elsewhere in Elizabeth City County eventually melded into one city, largely because of the unseen forces at work from Langley.

"The future of Hampton has rested in the expansion of the military," Quarstein said.

In 1916, the heralded seafood industry that had nourished Hampton for decades was in decline, according to local historian and retired University of Alabama professor Wythe Holt Jr.

The area's other major economic driver, the tourism attracted by huge hotels, such as the original Chamberlin Hotel at Fort Monroe, and Hampton's sandy beaches, was about to take a huge hit.

"The real main second industry after seafood was alcohol because the alcohol fueled the tourism," Holt said.

A statewide prohibition, passed in 1914, was set to take effect on Nov. 1, 1916. On that day, the many famed saloons of Phoebus that served the men stationed at Fort Monroe shut their doors.

But Holt's grandfather, Hampton Clerk of Court Harry Howard Holt, had a plan in motion. Pulling political strings, Holt attracted a forward-looking federal facility that had far-reaching effects on the area.

Into the modern age

With farming and aquaculture on the way out and the tourism business looking at a dry spell, the overhaul at Langley Field was the epicenter for a transformation in Hampton's economy.

"By the time the industries start to leave us, the future comes. The future knocks on the door. It brings prosperity; a lot of money comes from Washington, from NACA/NASA, from the Air Force," Cobb said. "When Langley and later NACA comes, it brings Hampton into the modern age."

Langley and NACA attracted technically skilled people. Some were traditionally educated engineers and mathematicians, while others were pilots and mechanics — most of whom made a lot more money than the farmers and crabbers living in Elizabeth City County.

ATTITUDES ON RACE

The arrival of Langley Field sparked many dramatic shifts, but some attitudes didn't change quite as much as some might think, according to local historian Wythe Holt Jr.

Holt said many today would think the highly educated workers who were coming through Langley would bring progressive political views, but there wasn't a major revolution in local politics at the time.

"Those folks were not necessarily liberals — there were lots of political viewpoints," Holt said.

Particularly, issues of race weren't immediately propelled forward just because of the people being brought to Langley Field from the North and Midwest.

"Integration was not a part of their agenda," he said, referring to the process of merging black and white populations that had been segregated, perhaps most visibly in schools explicitly reserved for black or white

Quarstein says getting from point A to point B in Hampton also underwent a virtual revolution with the advent of Langley Field. Hampton had to extend King Street to the gate of Langley, and the LaSalle and Mercury corridors also are products of the need to move people — largely military personnel — around the Peninsula. More often than not, point A was Fort Monroe and point B was Langley.

The extension of King Street also paved the way for Hampton's suburban development.

"Really after World War I is where you see the tremendous suburban growth that outpaces everything else that ever happened from a housing standpoint in Hampton and Newport News," Quarstein said.

Places such as Riverdale and Elizabeth Lakes were built to satisfy a newfound need for housing.

"The flyboys had to live somewhere. The NASA people had to live somewhere. Most of them lived here. ... These were folks who, essentially, could afford it because they worked for the government," Holt said. "Suburbs bloomed around here. We became much more urban and much less rural."

But it wasn't just undeveloped corridors that got a boost — the students.

Views on race relations didn't shift significantly within the community until much later, though historian and author John V. Quarstein said the tempering influence of Langley and the Department of Defense helped ease the transition in the 1950s.

"One of the biggest things is the acceptance of integration. The military insisted on it. Hampton does not close its schools in 1957. Hampton starts a slow process that will eventually be integration," Quarstein said.

In 1955, the Air Force took over the operation of an elementary school at Langley to comply with a 1954 order from the secretary of defense that forced the integration of all Department of Defense schools.

That elementary school became the first to integrate in Hampton.

According to Daily Press archives, Hampton was one of the first school systems in the state to desegregate and did so without a court order or lawsuit.

Hampton's public schools were fully integrated by the mid-1960s while other districts dragged their feet.

Ryan Murphy

towns of Hampton and Phoebus suddenly were flush with federal money.

As families moved in, the need for schools increased. Hampton's educational atmosphere was forced to keep up with the steady stream of children coming from families associated with the new air base, opening more and better public schools, Quarstein said.

"If you think about the impact of these military bases, you just have to look toward road construction, school construction, educated workforce," Quarstein said. "Whenever you have an improved workforce, it changes the upward mobility of a community and it strengthens the growth of new industries in the area."

Culture shock

The social climate and some modes of thinking shifted dramatically when personnel for Langley, and later NACA, arrived en masse.

"There was a social clash because as these newcomers came in, the locals stepped back a little bit because the engineers and such were very precise and there were all kinds of stories about the engineers and their different style of living," Cobb said. "There was a

This May 22, 1918, photo shows the first completed permanent brick hangar, top center, at Langley Field, as well as temporary metal hangars in various states of completion. *Air Combat Command History Office photo*

whole different language of technology that before this was really not familiar in Hampton. This language of engineering and technology was a far stretch from the language and the culture of the water and of the land.

"This cutting-edge culture of innovation was just far different from what existed before."

Different names for the educated engineers and mathematicians who started popping up in local hardware stores and corner grocers — "eggheads" and "NACA nuts" were two favorites — were tossed around by locals. It was half humor and half derision, but the casual interactions between scientists and pilots and native Hamptonians left an indelible impression.

Holt recalled one instance when famed German rocket scientist Wernher von Braun — a one-time Nazi scooped up by Americans in the aftermath of the fall of Berlin who became known as the father of modern rocketry — came to speak to his eighth-grade class at George Wythe Junior High School in the mid-1950s.

And it wasn't just young students in science classes being dazzled. The young women of Hampton and Phoebus suddenly had new dating options when relocated bachelors with government paychecks in their pockets descended on the area's dance halls.

"It brought in eligible males in their 20s who were going to be flyboys and provided a great deal of leavening for the local social and genetic scene," Holt said. "Grandview, I think, grew up in no small part because of this — they had a dance hall at Grandview."

"There were a lot of things for them to do locally and it made a more melded civilization. Less insulated. Less still fighting the Civil War," Holt said. "This helped overcome the antagonism toward the North."

Social interaction with people from across the country, predominantly from the Midwest and Northeast, altered the outlook of many in the area.

This was far from the first time Yankees had come to Hampton. Following the Civil War, many who arrived to establish the seafood industry were from north of the Mason-Dixon Line, so there had been exposure, but tensions remained.

Hampton, which Holt calls a "dyed-in-the-wool" Southern town, viewed the town of Phoebus with hostility.

"The then-town of Hampton had its greatest enemy in the town of Phoebus — a town born of the Union army occupation and an extension of Fort Monroe," Holt said.

The coming of the NACA people eventually eased these local tensions.

Before long, marriages between locals and the newcomers made NACA and Air Force personnel an integral part of the social and political landscape in Hampton.

"They didn't come with a vision to change things — the fact that they were here changed things," Cobb said. "(Langley Field) changed the entire tenor of Hampton, and all for the better."

One of the 94th Fighter Squadron's most famous members was "ace of aces" Eddie Rickenbacker, shown here during World War I. *U.S. Air Force file photo*

Storied squadrons

By Hugh Lessig

Together, the 27th and 94th fighter squadrons at Langley Air Force Base pack a significant punch for U.S. air power. Separately, the pilots always have maintained a friendly rivalry, pushing each other to be better.

And it's been going on for a while. Consider September 1918.

The scene was France, where World War I had shifted into high gear. Pilots of the 27th and 94th aero squadrons — the precursors of today's units — were in the thick of the fight. On Sept. 25, a new commander took over the 94th: Eddie Rickenbacker, America's "ace of aces," who would go on to become a household name.

The 94th had arrived in France before the 27th; its pilots had more combat experience. Upon taking over the 94th, Rickenbacker found a statistic that seemed a bit irksome: The 27th had taken the lead from the 94th in total kills. This was due in no small measure to the 27th's own knight of the air, Lt. Frank Luke, the "Arizona Balloon Buster," who would posthumously receive the Medal of Honor after his heroic death.

Capt. Eddie Rickenbacker, American ace fighter pilot, is shown with his Spad fighter plane during World War I. Rickenbacker served in the U.S. Air Service in France as commanding officer of the 94th Aero Pursuit Squadron. *U.S. Army Air Force photo*

After looking at the statistics, Rickenbacker gathered his pilots and declared that "no other American squadron at the front would ever again be permitted to approach our margin of supremacy."

Then he had a talk with the 94th's mechanics. He reported they "felt the disgrace of being second more keenly than did we the pilots."

This story comes from a history of the 1st Tactical Fighter Wing, now designated the 1st Fighter Wing, written by Charles F. O'Connell Jr. and published in 1987. It was provided to the Daily Press from Air Combat Command headquarters at Langley.

O'Connell's 180-page study draws on government documents, histories, a war diary and other sources. Combined with other texts provided by ACC, it tells the story of two squadrons that trace their lineage to the early days of U.S. combat aviation, each racking up an impressive list of honors along the way.

DARING, LESSER-KNOWN ACE

In World War I, fighter pilot Eddie Rickenbacker became America's "ace of aces," flying for the forerunner of today's 94th Fighter Squadron.

But a pilot for a rival American squadron also proved his mettle. He went down firing and died a hero.

Lt. Frank Luke earned the nickname of "Arizona Balloon Buster" for his daring attacks on heavily defended enemy observation balloons. In the fall of 1918, Luke flew alone to shoot down enemy balloons along the front, according to a history written by Charles F. O'Connell Jr.

In characteristic fashion, he destroyed two balloons, two German fighters and then a third balloon. But then, badly wounded and with a damaged plane, he made a forced landing. German troops were sent to capture him.

Luke drew his pistol and fired on the enemy. He died in the ensuing gun battle and for his actions received the Medal of Honor.

In Luke's online biography listed in the National Aviation Hall of Fame, Rickenbacker offered this tribute:

"He was the most daring aviator and greatest fighter pilot of the entire war. His life is one of the brightest glories of our Air Service. He went on a rampage and shot down 14 enemy aircraft, including 10 balloons, in eight days. No other Ace: Britain's (Billy) Bishop from Canada, France's (Rene) Fonck or even the dreaded Richthofen (the Red Baron) had ever come close to that."

Hugh Lessig

Joshua Lashley, 1st Fighter Wing historian, said the friendly competition between these two storied squadrons "makes them both stronger."

"The heritage of these two squadrons sets the standard for the rest of the Air Force," he said.

Neither unit began at Langley. In fact, the squadrons did not arrive until the mid-1970s along with the rest of the 1st Fighter Wing.

The unit that became the 27th organized on May 8, 1917, at Kelly Field in Texas, but it was under a different name. It was renamed the 27th Aero Squadron a few weeks later in June.

The 94th was organized shortly afterward, on Aug. 20, also at Kelly Field, where tens of thousands of Americans were joining the war effort.

'MALONEY'S PONY'

In honor of Lt. Frank Maloney, the highest-scoring ace of the 27th Fighter Squadron, the squadron in 2011 unveiled an F-22 Raptor with a pony logo. Shown here is a Raptor from a Langley air show in April 2016. *Daily Press file photo*

The history of both units is inextricably tied to the 1st Fighter Wing, which also traces its origins to WWI, where it was known as the 1st Pursuit Group. It was actually formed after the squadrons began fighting, when the military decided it needed larger umbrella organizations to group its smaller units in some order.

The 94th was first to arrive in France and, on March 6, 1918, launched the first patrol flown by an all-American squadron, even if it only consisted of two aircraft with no armament, led by an experienced French pilot.

A consignment of machine guns finally arrived in April. On April 14, "the pilots of the 94th stood alert as an active combat squadron for the first time," O'Connell writes.

Pilots of the 27th joined the fight in May.

"The 94th took over the task of introducing the 27th to the in-

Lt. Frank Maloney ended World War II as the highest-scoring ace of the 27th Fighter Squadron, which is now based at Langley Air Force Base in Hampton.

But he almost didn't make it home.

In 1944, Maloney ran into trouble while on a mission with his twin-engine P-38 Lightning. On a strafing run, he lost one engine to enemy ground fire. The second engine gave out as he tried to return to base. He ditched his aircraft a few miles off the French coast and quietly floated to shore, where he waited until dawn.

The beach had been mined, but over time the sand had shifted and the surface looked normal. Maloney was careful as he moved inland, but he still triggered a mine. He survived but with both legs injured.

For the next 10 days, he crawled along, eating little and drinking water from his canteen. Finally, he was rescued by the French.

According to information obtained from Langley, which described Maloney's mission, his return flight home was memorable, too. A dozen aircraft from the 27th escorted Maloney's plane as it flew out over the Mediterranean. Then they peeled away individually and returned to the war.

In honor of Maloney, it was ordered that airplane No. 23 should be forever named "Maloney's Pony." The Air Force no longer uses this numbering system, but in 2011, the 27th Fighter Squadron honored Maloney by unveiling an F-22 Raptor with a pony logo.

Hugh Lessig

tricacies of aerial combat," O'Connell wrote, "and pilots from the 94th led pilots of the 27th on their first patrols on 2 June (1918)."

Perhaps that made Rickenbacker's frustration a bit more understandable when it came to the number of kills.

(A proviso: The 27th and 94th squadrons were in the first wave of American-trained units to fight in the air war. They were not the first Americans. That honor belonged to the American volunteers of the Lafayette Escadrille, who fought against the Germans before the U.S. declared war.)

The two squadrons emerged from World War I with their own storylines: Rickenbacker's "Hat in the Ring Gang," probably the most famous of the units, while the "Fighting Eagles" of the 27th were the older of the two.

Insignia backstories

The hat in the ring squadron flag was on display at Langley Air Force Base in 2007 in honor of the 94th Fighter Squadron's 90th birthday. *Daily Press file photo*

The 27th Fighter Squadron continues to use a variation of the original design dating back to 1918.
1st Fighter Wing public affairs office

As for which unit has the better insignia, that's probably in the eye of the beholder. But each one has an interesting story.

The 94th's emblem shows Uncle Sam's hat in the middle of a ring. As O'Connell tells it, the design grew from discussions of those WWI pilots.

The 94th's commanding officer, Maj. John F. Huffler, suggested the Uncle Sam tall hat. Lt. Paul Walters, the squadron medical officer, suggested throwing the hat into a ring to symbolize the U.S. entry into the war after initially staying neutral. Thus, the hat in the ring was born.

But it didn't stay that way. After the war, the famous Rickenbacker decided to produce and sell automobiles that bore his name. He adopted the hat in the ring logo for this company.

The Air Force didn't want to be seen as promoting a commercial product, so it changed to an Indian-head insignia that also had an honorable tradition, being tied to the Lafayette Escadrille. That stood until 1942 when Rickenbacker, on a tour of flying World War II units, linked up with the 94th and was asked what had become of the famous hat in the ring insignia. Couldn't they get it back?

Rickenbacker took that request up the chain, and the old logo was reassigned.

Pilots of the 27th had this same discussion in 1918. They reportedly tossed around a few possibilities before Lt. Malcolm Gunn said he happened to like the logo of Anheuser-Busch brewery, which incorporated an eagle in its design. A corporal drew a variation on that theme — an eagle with spread wings, talons out, diving on its prey.

A falcon replaced the eagle in 1924, as the Air Force decided it did not wish to be seen as endorsing a brewery. Today, the 27th continues to use a variation of the original design.

A phosphorus bomb explodes over the USS Alabama during a Sept. 27, 1921, demonstration carried out by bombers from Langley Field. *Naval History and Heritage Command photo*

Bombs away!

By Mark St. John Erickson

Brig. Gen. William "Billy" Mitchell was no stranger to Hampton Roads when he formed the 1st Provisional Air Brigade at Langley Field in the spring of 1921.

Five years earlier, he'd taken the overnight steamer from Washington, D.C., to Old Point Comfort nearly every fall weekend, then driven from the Hotel Chamberlin to the Curtiss Flying School at Newport News to take private flying lessons and — at the relatively advanced age of 36 — earn his pilot's wings.

He reportedly went gunning for ducks on the Back River during the fall of 1916, too — just when his superiors in the Aviation Section of the Signal Corps were inspecting the property along its banks as a possible site for the Army's first purpose-built airfield.

But returning to Langley as deputy chief of the newly organized Air Service in 1921, the ambitious aviator — who had commanded legions of Allied planes in World War I — was intent on proving the combat value of a weapon still widely and stubbornly dismissed by such figures as Assistant Secretary of the Navy Franklin D. Roosevelt.

Mobilizing the young airmen of Langley's pioneering Air Service Tactical School, Mitchell instituted a revolutionary training pro-

Brig. Gen. William "Billy" Mitchell was an outspoken advocate of air power. *U.S. Air Force photo*

gram designed to pit aerial bombs against seemingly impregnable battleships, which most strategists of the day saw as the nation's best coastal defense.

"Billy Mitchell was a very controversial figure. But he knew what he was doing," said John V. Quarstein, author of "World War I on the Virginia Peninsula," sizing up the historic demonstrations in which the visionary general and his fliers destroyed the 27,000-ton German dreadnought Ostfriesland and three obsolete American battleships.

"He saw the future of warfare. And the Langley planes proved him right."

Insurgent aims

Just two years removed from the threat of closing after WWI, Langley still was making the transition from farms and woods to a pioneering military air installation when Mitchell began commuting from Washington.

Much of the property surrounding its newly completed dirigible and balloon hangar remained planted in crops, while the Back River teemed with work boats.

"It is indeed an interesting picture to see the airplanes circling overhead," Maj. Thomas DeWitt Milling observed, "while the oystermen are industriously planting their oysters in the blue waters of this picturesque stream."

Still, most of the permanent structures started in 1917 and then bogged down by delays during the war had been completed, giving a distinctive architectural identity to a place that famed Detroit architect Albert Kahn and Langley's founders, including Milling — a member of the original site selection board — had envisioned as an Army aviation hub like no other.

Though temporary buildings erected in haste during the war still abounded, the field ranked as the nation's largest.

Brig. Gen. William "Billy" Mitchell, at center with arm raised, briefs Gen. John J. Pershing, to his left, and Secretary of War John W. Weeks, center left, on the Martin MB-2 bomber before the 1921 bombing demonstrations off the Virginia Capes. *Air Combat Command History Office photo*

It also had embraced its new mission as the aerial defender of the Chesapeake Bay and the approaches to Washington, D.C., in ways that restored some of its original ambition, becoming what Milling — who ranked as the service's first rated pilot — championed as "undoubtedly the finest airplane landing field on the entire Atlantic Coast."

Among its most enterprising innovations after the war's end was the groundbreaking Tactical School, which Milling founded in July 1920 to indoctrinate the Air Service's officers in aerial tactics, aeronautical engineering and administration.

Its classrooms explored such subjects as observation, pursuit, bombardment, meteorology, navigation, photography, communications and law, with the later addition of anti-aircraft defense and balloon and airship flying.

No aspect of its training regime was more influential, however, than the experience the class of 1920-21 gained after being recruited by Mitchell to demonstrate the superiority of the airplane over battleships.

Milling and his instructors welcomed the daring challenge, believing that the practical benefits of the exercises known as "Proj-

35

A TRADITION OF DEMOS

Visitors view a B-17 Flying Fortress during an open house at Langley Air Force Base in 1945. Langley has a long history of demonstrations of U.S. air power for the public's benefit. *Air Combat Command History Office photo*

ect B" would have far greater value than anything they could teach their students in the classroom.

"This is a very small cadre of individuals — and the Air Service is grooming them as its future leaders," said William M. Butler, deputy command historian of the Air Combat Command.

"Basically, Mitchell co-opts them for these bombing demonstrations. He never had an order assigning him to this mission."

All wrought up

Outspoken and abrasive, Mitchell had pushed passionately for the development of air power after the war, arguing not only that a thousand bombers could be built at the cost of a single battleship but also that those planes could then turn around and bomb any battleship into oblivion.

Langley Air Force Base has been home to demonstrations of U.S. air power for decades, and it always has been for the public's benefit.

In the years following World War I, interest in the emerging aviation industry as a tool of war was sky high. The 1st Pursuit Group — the forerunner of today's 1st Fighter Wing — staged a number of events that served a twofold purpose for the War Department. It was good public relations, and it just might impress a few taxpaying citizens and members of Congress along the way.

On March 5, 1925, a demonstration was held at Langley Field, where congressmen were allowed to inspect the planes up close. That afternoon, a dozen planes launched a simulated attack on a battleship silhouette. First came strafing, then light bombs, then fighters laid a smoke screen to cover another attack.

"The spectators seemed duly impressed with this demonstration," according to a history of the group written by Charles F. O'Connell Jr., "but some contact with members of Congress brought the group rather less favorable attention."

Later that month in Pennsylvania, a pilot from the Pursuit Group crashed shortly after takeoff from an airfield near Uniontown. The pilot was not hurt, but his passenger suffered a broken collarbone and several broken ribs. That passenger happened to a member of Congress.

"The congressman's reaction to this mishap is not recorded ..." O'Connell wrote.

Hugh Lessig

Though the Navy had taken the lead in the dispute with its systematic bombing tests of the obsolete battleship USS Indiana in October 1920, it still required numerous sensational news stories and the subsequent urging of Congress to persuade the secretaries of war and Navy to sign off on a second series of tests, which the Navy agreed to stage with the Air Service's participation about 50 miles off the Virginia Capes.

Beginning that March, Mitchell and Milling — who assumed responsibility for organizing the provisional brigade — initiated a demanding training regime in which their airmen practiced over land and water during daylight and darkness, wrote Air Force historians Robert I. Curtis, John Mitchell and Martin Copp in their 1977 book "Langley Field: The Early Years 1916-1946."

Automobiles driving down Langley's roads simulated moving

targets, as did dummy targets towed through the nearby water.

Then there was the silhouette of a battleship marked out on the bombing range at Mulberry Island.

In addition to Langley's Tactical School students, bombers and airships, the brigade included airmen from Kelly Field in Texas and Mitchel Field, N.Y., all of whom toiled to perfect their strafing, bombing and observation skills, as well as newly developed aerial tactics for attacking vessels.

"It took a lot of practice before they actually dropped a big one," Butler says, describing the progression from sand bags to 2,000-pound bombs newly designed to kill ships.

"But they worked out all the details that we refer to today as 'Tactics, Techniques and Procedures.'"

So keen were the Army fliers to prove their mettle that many pleaded with the Air Service "to settle the matter under honest to goodness wartime conditions," with "the fleet ... allowed to fire back at them with anti-aircraft guns," the March 28, 1921, Aviation and Aircraft Journal reported.

Some pilots pointed out the significance of the test site's proximity to Hampton Roads, where the USS Monitor and CSS Virginia had changed naval history through the first clash of ironclad warships during the Civil War.

"They have been all wrought up ... since that not distant day when Josephus Daniels, then Secretary of the Navy, offered to stand bare-headed on the deck of a battleship and let Brig. Gen. Mitchell, head of the air service in the war, take a crack at him with bombing planes," the journal noted.

Cooler heads prevailed, but it's clear that Mitchell had won the hearts of the Army's flying corps, who embraced his theories as gospel.

"We have this shot with Mitchell standing in the middle of the field, looking up and orchestrating this big review, where they're parading all their planes around in the sky," Butler said, describing a photo taken the day the bombing trials started.

"It's a huge demonstration of American air power."

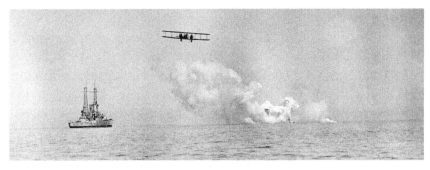

Top: A Martin bomber from Langley Field lays down a screen of smoke during bombing demonstrations in September 1921 targeting the USS Alabama off the Virginia Capes. **Middle**: The ship is hit by a phosphorus bomb from a Langley plane. **Bottom:** Inspectors view the damage from the bombing. *Air Combat Command History Office photos*

Bombs away

The tests began on June 21, 1921, in the Atlantic Fleet training grounds off the Virginia Capes — where three Navy F-5L flying boats from Naval Air Station Norfolk stunned observers by sinking the German submarine U-117 in only 16 minutes.

Two waves of Langley bombers attacked the German destroyer G-102 on July 13, sinking it with 300-pound bombs after strafing runs by pursuit planes.

"Langley Air Demons Send Old Hun Destroyer to Davy's Locker in 17 Minutes," the Daily Press reported.

The German cruiser Frankfort provided the target July 18 but stubbornly refused to sink after two attacks with 250-, 300- and 550-pound bombs — some of them delivered by Navy torpedo-bombers based at Aviation Field Yorktown — smashed its super-structure.

Stopping to assess the damage, Army and Navy inspectors agreed that further attacks would be futile.

Then six Langley planes made a final sortie with 600-pound bombs.

"Two hit cruiser's deck and third, exploding alongside, breaks her back," The New York Times reported, describing a deliberate near-miss that sent the ship to the bottom in minutes.

Still, the main event didn't take place until the July 20 and 21 assaults on the battleship Ostfriesland, a 27,000-ton behemoth that had survived 18 direct hits from heavy British naval guns and a clash with a high-explosive mine.

Conducted by Navy and Army planes using 230-, 550- and 600-pound bombs, the first day's attacks were ineffectual, The New York Times reported.

They also came near to marking the last flight of the Air Service's frustrated deputy chief. Developing engine trouble on the way home, Mitchell was forced to land unceremoniously in a muddy ditch in Virginia Beach, then Princess Anne County.

Only after digging the plane out and repairing the engine did he and Streett return to Langley Field, "very muddy and worn out but none the worse for their trip ... (to) general elation among the fli-

Langley airships move into position to observe the bombing demonstrations conducted off the Virginia Capes beginning in June 1921. At center is the battleship Ostfriesland, the target for the tests. *Naval History and Heritage Command photo*

ers," the Daily Press reported.

A second wave of attacks launched the following day seemed doomed to failure, too, partly because of the Navy's previously agreed-to focus on systematically assessing the damage inflicted by each bomb that struck the ship or scored a near miss capable of smashing the hull.

Knowing his planes could not stay in the air long enough to deliver repeated punches, Mitchell instructed them to strike before the Navy airmen from Yorktown, scheduled to lead the assault with newly developed armor-piercing bombs, arrived.

He also ordered his pilots to drop most of their 2,000-pound bombs at once rather than allowing the attack to be interrupted for the inspections.

The huge ship shuddered under the impact of the intentional near misses, which smashed through its hull below the waterline and sank it in 22 minutes.

"We could see her rise 8 to 10 feet between the terrific blows from under water," said Mitchell, who directed the attacks from his de Havilland 4, named the Osprey.

"On the fourth shot, Capt. Streett, sitting in the back of my plane, stood up and waving both arms shouted: 'She is gone!' "

FIGHTER LIKE NO OTHER

Langley's first F/A-22 Raptor arrives in May 2005 with pilot Lt. Col. Jim Hecker, 27th Fighter Squadron commander, at the controls. *Daily Press file photos*

Signal triumph

Aboard the USS Henderson, some Navy men in the crowd of admirals, generals, congressmen and journalists looking on broke down in tears, Mitchell later noted in his 1925 book "Winged Defense."

But he still buzzed them with a defiant wave of his wings, certain that he and his fliers had proven the superiority of air power.

Still, despite the Ostfriesland's demise and the later sinking of three obsolete American battleships by Langley planes, the argument was far from settled.

Mitchell later would be demoted, exiled to Texas and then court-martialed in 1925 because of the tactless zeal with which he pressed his views, including his sensational prophecy of another world war and the Japanese bombing of the American fleet at Pearl Harbor, Hawaii.

Even such conservative observers as Army ordnance chief Maj. Gen. C.C. Williams saw that Langley airmen had scored a landmark triumph.

"A bomb was fired today that will be heard around the world," he said.

"It is a heavier explosive charge than has ever been delivered

As early as 2000, the Air Force's first choice for the operational home of the F-22 Raptor was Langley Air Force Base and the 1st Fighter Wing. But not until 2002 did the service make that pick official — and not until May 12, 2005, did the stealthy Lockheed Martin aircraft finally land and taxi to newly constructed hangars, just in time to strut their stuff at the air base's 2005 air power show.

Then and now, the Air Force calls the plane unmatched as an air superiority fighter.

"There are limitless possibilities as to what these aircraft can do," Maj. Kevin Dolata, chief of the 1st Fighter Wing's Raptor integration program, told the Daily Press just days before the first F-22s landed.

"We can't kick the door down if we don't own the sky."

Mark St. John Erickson

against a battleship. Its sinking of the Ostfriesland means that the capital ship now faces a new menace that must be guarded against by every possible study and effort."

Langley fliers celebrated their milestone kill with far less reserve, convinced by Mitchell and their own exploits that the airplane was the weapon of the future.

"This was the practical application of all the theoretical possibilities they'd been studying at the Tactical School," Butler said.

"They were applying pure air power in a way it hadn't been applied before — uncoordinated with any other kind of force — and they were just cutting their teeth."

The 410-foot-long Roma has a crowd of spectators and ground crew at Langley Field during the giant airship's Nov. 15, 1921, maiden voyage. *Daily Press file photo*

Leviathan's fiery end

By Mark St. John Erickson

Midway through the morning of Nov. 15, 1921, an eye-popping sight rose into the skies over Langley Field.

At 410 feet long, the airship Roma was a leviathan — the largest lighter-than-air craft in the world.

And for more than three hours, the mammoth machine sailed over the lower Peninsula on its first American flight, commanding the attention and occasional disbelief of thousands.

Just 13 weeks later, the Italian-built dirigible would crash in a fiery and broken heap, killing 34 airmen in a catastrophe so horrific and grisly that reports of twisted wreckage and charred remains darkened the Daily Press for days.

But its historic maiden voyage was steeped in grace, glory and wonder.

"How did we look when we left the ground?" the Roma's wireless operator asked as the ship sailed over the Back River to the Chesapeake Bay, then turned south toward Old Point Comfort and Fort Mon-

This 1921 photo shows the giant airship Roma emerging from its 420-foot-long hangar, which cost more than $400,000 to construct, about $5.2 million today. *Daily Press file photo*

roe.

"Magnificent!" an airman on the ground replied, echoing the breathless crowd that looked up from the ground beside the massive hangar, including a Daily Press reporter who called the aerial marvel "a sight that will linger with all who witnessed it."

"Balloons were the first aviation observation platforms — and in 1922, they still hadn't been outstripped by airplanes. They could stay aloft longer. They had a higher ceiling. They could maintain their position almost indefinitely. They could carry much more ordnance," said Deputy Command Historian William M. Butler of Air Combat Command at what is now Langley Air Force Base.

"All those advantages were driving the Air Service to explore and experiment with their potential."

High ambition

Though the Army operated tethered observation balloons in World War I, it had no self-propelled dirigibles, and it was eager to catch up with other nations.

"The Europeans — and especially the Germans — had quite a bit of success with lighter-than-air ships during the war," says Command Historian Mike Dugre, citing the landmark Zeppelin bombing raids over Paris and London.

"So it was still seen as a viable platform worth spending money on."

Even before the war's end, the first permanent structure erected at Langley Field was a hydrogen gas generating and compressor plant, which rose from the grounds of ancient Lamington Plantation in 1917.

Two years later, workmen began building a huge lighter-than-air hangar that measured 420 feet long, 125 feet wide and 116 feet high.

A pair of sunken rails extended 780 feet from its immense front doors, enabling tractors to pull out a towering mast designed for airship docking.

Finished in late 1921, the giant structure cost $426,550 — equal to $5.2 million today — and loomed over everything else.

"It was huge," Butler said, "almost like another base."

Much of the drive for the program came from Deputy Air Service Chief Brig. Gen. William "Billy" Mitchell, who returned from the war believing that airships had an important role to play in the unfolding realm of military aviation.

He pushed even harder when Italy began exploring dirigibles as both aircraft carriers and platforms for launching long-distance attacks with radio-controlled aerial torpedoes.

"When you think of all the things that Zeppelins could do — and that planes couldn't do back then — you can see why they were so interested in lighter-than-air," said John V. Quarstein, author of "World War I on the Virginia Peninsula."

"To a lot of people, it looked like the future."

Italian dirigible the world's largest

Langley's first airship was the 162-foot-long A4, a single-engine craft that arrived in July 1919 with a top speed of 45 mph.

Then there was the Pony Blimp, whose much smaller heft came with outsized handling problems.

"(It) took a notion to act like a full-grown horse and broke away from its moorings," an Air Service newsletter reported in 1921.

"(It) began a very violent fit of bucking that threw Maj. Fisher and Lt. Burt from the gondola, and then started on a wild race to the sea, carrying Master Sgt. McNally along with it."

Though Mitchell's attempts to buy a Zeppelin were thwarted, he

47

acquired several other foreign airships.

They included two British Sea Scout Twins and the French-built ZDUS-1, a 262-foot-long craft with two 220-horsepower engines capable of reaching 50 mph.

But they all looked puny beside the 410-foot Roma, whose six 450-horsepower Ansaldo engines could surpass 65 mph, write Air Force historians in the 1977 book "Langley Field: The Early Years 1916-1946."

Purchased in June 1920 for $194,000, the Italian dirigible was the world's largest airship — and the first flown by the American armed services.

Eight Langley airmen traveled to Italy to take delivery in early 1921, carefully inspecting the craft and testing it in flight before disassembling and packing it up for shipment.

Soon after the huge crates arrived at Langley on Aug. 10, 1921, the reassembly work started.

Though an Air Service newsletter described the Roma as being "in excellent condition in every respect," a later report called the fabric envelope "excessively mildewed" and so riddled with holes it needed nearly 200 patches.

Still, no leaks were detected when Langley airmen tested it Nov. 15, after which the Daily Press reported they were "elated over the behavior of the big ship from the time the balloon began to leave the ground until it was again snugly placed back in its immense hangar."

"We are sailing very nicely and everything is well," the wireless operator said.

"The weather conditions are grand."

Deadly descent

When the Roma returned to Langley, it took a ground crew of more than 300 to secure its landing ropes and maneuver the giant craft into its hangar.

Newsreel photographers who recorded the sight rushed to their lab, then to the Imperial Theatre in Newport News, where footage of the successful flight thrilled the evening's audiences.

"The sailing of the ship in the air was as peaceful and calm as if the

Ground crew members grab ropes while mechanics stand on the engine catwalks to work on the motors while readying for the Roma's first American flight on Nov. 15, 1921. It took a ground crew of more than 300 to secure the craft. *Air Combat Command History Office photo*

big dirigible had been in use for several years," the front page of the Daily Press proclaimed the next morning.

It moved through the skies "as gracefully and as prettily as the flying of the American eagle."

Behind the elated newsreels and headlines, however, the Roma's commander was frustrated by the balky Italian engines, which ran so poorly in cold weather that they caused the cancellation of a Dec. 9, 1921, christening ceremony at Bolling Field near Washington, D.C. — then a three-hour delay after the event was rescheduled.

"They were much too cold during the entire flight," Capt. Dale Mabry complained.

Even after the crew doused them with boiling water, "it was impossible to warm them up to running temperature."

Limping back to Langley, the Roma was grounded by the Chief of the Air Service until it could be refitted with lighter, more powerful Liberty engines.

The swap took six weeks to complete, and at 1:45 p.m. Feb. 21, 1922, the repowered craft rose into the air for a test flight.

Though it reached cruising speed quickly, its nose began to lose its shape even before the Roma turned south at the mouth of the Back River.

Witnesses in Phoebus later reported that it looked "crinkled up," while others at Willoughby Spit said it appeared "flattened."

Sailing over Hampton Roads toward Norfolk, the crew felt the ship shake momentarily at 2:15 p.m. after which the nose pitched down 45 degrees. Lt. Byron Burt struggled to right the Roma as it dropped, but the huge box elevator at the stern did not respond to his wheel.

Even after he ordered the engines cut — slowing the agonizingly slow yet disastrous descent — the crew's frantic efforts to lighten the ship by throwing ballast overboard proved futile.

"There was a rip and a roar. She plunged downward. We hit some wires. Flames burst out in several places," Burt reported in the following day's Daily Press.

"I think one end of the blimp reached the earth. There was a deafening explosion. That's all I remember."

Stunned response

Thirty-four airmen died in the crash, many burned beyond recognition by the devastating combination of ruptured gasoline tanks, flammable hydrogen gas and a 2,200-volt electric line.

But Burt and 10 others escaped the flames that rose 800 feet into the air by ripping their way through the ship's envelope as it crumpled into the ground.

"I jumped for this opening and with my bare hands tore away the flaming fabric," Maj. John D. Reardon told the Daily Press.

"Then I jumped out and fell on a pile of metal. I got up and ran. A man caught me, and I felt water splashed on my head and back.

"My clothing was burning. But I was still alive."

So loud was the explosion of the Roma that it could be heard as far away as Newport News and Langley Field.

Horrific reports from the scene added to the impact, stunning not just the Langley airmen but also the people of Hampton and New-

Spectators rush to the blazing airship Roma after it crashed and burned near Norfolk Naval Base. The blast could be heard 30 miles away at Langley Field. *Daily Press file photo*

Lt. Byron Burt looks over the wreckage of the Roma. Burt, who struggled to right the Roma, survived the crash that killed 34 airmen. *Air Combat Command History Office photo*

Somber faces reflect the task of searching for victims of the Roma crash. The Daily Press reported that the news of the crash shocked residents of Newport News and Hampton, where "practically every member of the Roma party was known." *Daily Press file photo*

port News, where "practically every member of the Roma party was known," the paper reported.

Thousands lined up to watch the half-mile-long funeral procession make its way through downtown Newport News, while businesses, courts and government offices across the Peninsula paused at noon in silent tribute to the victims and their families.

Airplanes from Langley circled overhead during the solemn ceremony, then swept in from the east, raining flowers on the somber crowd and the solitary flag-draped coffin that represented the dead.

"Navigation of the air is a science as yet in the experimental stage," the editorial page of the Daily Press intoned, trying to explain what ranked as the nation's deadliest aviation disaster until the Hindenburg crashed 15 years later.

"The experiments involve risk of life and limb, but the men of the (air) service are nothing deterred ...

"Those who survive will go right on with their work."

Firemen, rescuers and spectators work at the scene of the Roma crash. *Daily Press file photo*

A service for the Roma's fallen airmen in Newport News drew thousands four days after the disaster killed 34 airmen. *Daily Press file photo*

A flight of B-17s from Langley Field, which took the lead in testing the iconic craft and pioneering long-distance flying during the late 1930s. *Air Combat Command History Office photo*

B-17s blaze trail

By Mark St. John Erickson

When the first B-17 bombers took off from Langley Field in 1937, the giant experimental planes filled the skies over Hampton Roads with a warlike rumble never heard before.

Most of that deafening roar came from their mighty Cyclone 9 engines, which generated as much as 24,000 horsepower all told and introduced the menacing aerial sound that became a World War II icon.

But some small part may have been the defiant growls of the rebellious Langley airmen, who had embraced the new Flying Fortress as their most promising weapon in a bitter war for independence.

Championed by Brig. Gen. Frank M. Andrews — who founded General Headquarters Air Force at Langley in March 1935 — the massive aircraft and the revolutionary bombing doctrine it embodied were stubbornly resisted by the War Department's General Staff, who dismissed the B-17 and the ideas behind it as "Andrews'

Brig. Gen. Frank M. Andrews founded the General Headquarters Air Force at Langley. *Daily Press file photo*

Folly."

But even after being sacked in 1939, then sent to the same remote Texas post that air power advocate Brig. Gen. William "Billy" Mitchell had been exiled to in 1925, Andrews' determined campaign to redefine the combat role of Army aviation proved prophetic.

Within four months, the one-time cavalryman was summoned to Washington, D.C., by new Chief of Staff Gen. George C. Marshall, who made Andrews his top aide after a crucial visit to Langley Field had convinced him of the airplane's importance.

And by the war's end, the strategic power of the B-17 had not only played a defining role in the Allied victory but also opened the final door to an independent Air Force.

"The B-17s come here first — starting this progression in which a lot of the officers who figured out how to use them become notable figures in World War II," said William M. Butler, deputy command historian of Air Combat Command at what is now Langley Air Force Base.

"The Air Force became the Air Force because of the ideas about air power and bombardment that get started here."

Air crusader

Despite the destructive capability proven by Mitchell and Langley fliers off the Virginia capes in 1921 and '23 — when they overturned the prevailing doctrine of battleship invincibility with a series of dramatic bombing trials — the Air Service remained a secondary arm of the Army well into the 1930s.

But molded by the insurrectionist views of Langley's Air Service Tactical School, its officers bristled at how the rapidly growing promise of air power routinely was belittled by the General Staff, which did not include any airmen.

56

On March 1, 1937, the first YB-17 arrives at Langley Field. The pilot, Maj. Barney M. Giles, is greeted by Lt. Gen. Frank M. Andrews, General Headquarters commander. Eleven more Flying Fortresses arrived in the following five months and were all assigned to the 2nd Bombardment Group. *Air Combat Command History Office photo*

"The Tactical School taught, and Air Corps officers as a rule believed, aviation could be decisive," writes Air Force historian Mauer Mauer in "Aviation in the U.S. Army 1919-1939."

"The General Staff and officers of the other arms could not accept this. ... As the War Plans Division put it: 'So far, well-organized nations have surrendered only when occupied by the enemy's army or when such occupation could no longer be opposed.' "

A 1928 graduate of the Tactical School, Andrews became a leading proponent of air power, writing on the airplane's role in national defense during later studies at the War College.

And like his fellow fliers, he was both impressed and disheartened by the pioneering flight of Italian Air Marshal Italo Balbo and a fleet of 24 flying boats in August 1933, when they flew from Italy to the U.S. and a triumphant welcome at the Chicago World's Fair.

Though the War Department dismissed the feat as a stunt, Andrews flew out with the 1st Pursuit Group from Selfridge Field near Detroit, greeting the Italians at the Canadian border with an aerial salute.

"Balbo and his men had clearly demonstrated that with proper aeronautical equipment and training, airmen would soon be able to fly long distances in adverse weather to reach any adversary's industrial heartland," writes DeWitt S. Copp in "Frank M. Andrews: Marshall's Airman."

"If the War Department failed to recognize what military leaders of other countries foresaw, U.S. air power could not keep pace. Andrews was determined to see this did not happen."

Power struggle

So poorly equipped and ill-trained was the Air Corps in early 1934 that when President Franklin D. Roosevelt commandeered it to carry the nation's airmail, it proved embarrassingly unequal to the task, losing a dozen airmen in weather-related crashes, Copp notes.

But the uproar in Congress led to a new board charged with charting the Corps' future — and a directive to reorganize that won support from Chief of Staff Gen. Douglas MacArthur.

Summoned to Washington, Andrews chaired the committee that recommended the creation of General Headquarters Air Force, which consolidated for the first time the command of all the Army's combat aviation units under a single officer.

Though such proposals had been quashed by the War Department since 1923, MacArthur not only agreed but also passed over 12 senior officers to make Andrews its commander.

He started with only 446 aircraft — just 176 of those classed as modern — and far short of the 980 the Army had approved, Copp writes.

He fielded fewer than half of the 1,245 pilots he needed and lagged just as badly in enlisted airmen.

Equally pressing was the need for a long-range heavy bomber capable of carrying out the independent combat missions that he and his officers saw as the defining role of an air force.

"Andrews is building on the ideas of Billy Mitchell and the airplane's power to penetrate deeply into the enemy heartland,"

A YB-17 arrives at Langley in this undated photo. *Air Combat Command History Office photo*

historian John V. Quarstein said.

"And for that he needed a bomber that could fly high, fly far and deliver a tremendous bomb load hundreds of miles away from its base."

Pioneer bombers

Developed in response to a guileful Air Corps' proposal — which tried to deflect critics by specifying a long-range bomber capable of defending Hawaii, Alaska and the Panama Canal — the Boeing B-17 was the largest and most advanced contender when it arrived for a fly-off at Wright Field in Ohio on Aug. 20, 1935.

Landing an hour early after a nonstop 2,100-mile flight from Seattle, the gleaming four-engine prototype flew longer, higher and — by averaging 232 mph — faster than its two-engine competitors, writes Phillip Mellinger in Air Force Magazine.

But when it stalled and crashed on a later takeoff after the crew failed to unlock its rudder and elevator controls, it was scrubbed from the trials, prompting Chief of Staff Gen. Malin Craig to cancel Andrews' preliminary order for 65 and fund 133 Douglas B-18

MORE THAN FIGHTER JETS

Fighter jets keep a high profile at Langley Air Force Base, but the installation is about more than aircraft.

For the record, its official name is Joint Base Langley Eustis, the result of a modified merger between Langley and Fort Eustis in Newport News, which was ordered as part of the 2005 Base Realignment and Closure commission.

Each base kept its separate identity, and the Daily Press still uses Langley Air Force Base and Fort Eustis to refer to the individual bases when possible because Joint Base Langley Eustis is not a physical location.

It also can be confusing. In October 2011, President Barack Obama announced plans to speak at Joint Base Langley Eustis. He actually spoke at the Air Force base in Hampton.

Here are the major units listed on the website for Langley, the only Air Force Base in Virginia and among the oldest continuously active air bases in the U.S.:

633rd Air Base Wing Mission: Its three groups support more than 9,000 military and civilian personnel. Its activation in January 2010 as the new host unit for Langley AFB was the first step toward Joint Base Langley

medium bombers instead.

Desperate to acquire the weapon they considered essential, Andrews and his allies in Congress and the Army exploited a loophole, enabling him to bring 12 Flying Fortresses to Langley for experimental testing.

The first arrived on March 1, 1937, and by August, the 2nd Bombardment Group could field an entire squadron.

"The B-17 would become one of the most successful aircraft in military aviation history," Quarstein said.

"And it all started here because of Andrews' vision and what he did at Langley."

Even before his 12th plane arrived, the GHQ commander staged an epic nonstop flight that spanned 20 cities and 1,200 miles, giving his fliers an unprecedented training exercise as well as national attention.

In February 1938, Col. Robert Olds — a key figure in the Air Corps' so-called "Bomber Mafia" — sparked still more headlines

Eustis.

Air Combat Command headquarters: Created in 1992 by combining Strategic Air Command and Tactical Air Command, ACC is the primary provider of air combat forces to America's war-fighting commanders.

1st Fighter Wing: The primary home for the F-22 Raptor, the wing includes the 27th and 94th fighter squadrons and the 71st Fighter Training Squadron, plus two maintenance squadrons.

192nd Fighter Wing: The Air National Guard component of the Virginia National Guard, this unit also flies and maintains the F-22.

480th Intelligence, Surveillance and Reconnaissance Wing: These airmen provide intelligence collected from manned and unmanned aircraft around the globe. The 480th oversees six ISR groups, including the 497th ISR group at Langley. The others are based in Georgia, California, Hawaii, Germany and South Korea.

363rd Intelligence, Surveillance and Reconnaissance Wing: Established in 2015, a major task of this sister ISR unit is to look through massive amounts of data churned out by the 480th and do long-term studies to determine trends. Its work is valuable to commanders who must assess risks of various missions.

Hugh Lessig

with a marathon 11,952-mile flight to and from Argentina.

Among his officers was Lt. Curtis E. LeMay, who previously had served as the lead navigator during an August 1937 exercise in which the B-17s — with Andrews on board — had located and "bombed" the USS Utah off the fog-shrouded California coast.

The future Air Force chief showed his skill again in March 1938, when he led Langley bombers from New York and — with NBC Radio, The New York Times and the New York Herald Tribune riding along — intercepted the Italian passenger liner Rex 700 miles out in the cloudy Atlantic.

Dramatic photographs of the B-17s flying over the ship appeared the next day on the front pages of newspapers around the world.

"Not only were they showing that they could sink ships far off the coast, but also that they could and maybe should be the force responsible for defending the coast," Butler said.

"They were really extending their mission."

Loss and legacy

Such public challenges to the status quo provoked mounting anger in Washington, which immediately ordered Andrews' bombers to venture no farther than 100 miles from land.

Six months later, Gen. Craig offered to make his rebellious officer the chief of the Air Corps if he would drop the B-17, but Andrews refused, Copp writes.

That probably sealed his fate — and he may have felt like he had nothing more to lose when his description of the U.S. as a "sixth-rate air power" made national headlines in January 1939.

"There were few dry eyes," Copp reports, describing the anger and sorrow of Andrews' airmen at his farewell Langley review, after which he was posted to Mitchell's old place of banishment in Texas.

Still, his exile lasted only until Craig retired in July 1939, when the personal, nine-day tour Andrews had given the previous year to Brig. Gen. Marshall, then the War Plans chief, paid a landmark dividend.

Swayed by the tremendous advances in capability and training he saw as Andrews piloted him from field to field, the new chief of staff fought to make the defiant airman his top aide — and the first flier on the General Staff.

"Under our present scheme ... the operating personnel have very little contact with the powers that be," Andrews had told his new boss. "We know our stuff, but we cannot get it across."

With the nation's entry into World War II, Marshall not only listened but also entrusted Andrews with increasingly important missions, including reorganizing the defense of the Caribbean and the Panama Canal and leading American forces in the Middle East.

He was chief of U.S. forces in Europe when he died in a May 3, 1943, plane crash.

Four months earlier, however, Andrews' determined belief in the power of the B-17 and long-range strategic bombing had been confirmed by the Allies' decision to mount a devastating, if costly, air offensive against Germany.

By the war's end, his original Langley squadron of 12 B-17s had spawned the production of more than 12,700 others.

And his long crusade for an independent Air Force finally triumphed in 1947.

"Today, when American bombers fly a successful mission in any theater of war, their achievement goes back to the blueprints of the General Headquarters Air Force," wrote Henry H. "Hap" Arnold, head of Army Air Forces and first General of the Air Force, praising Andrews and his crucial Langley legacy.

"Our operations were based on the needs and problems of our own hemisphere, with its vast seas, huge land areas, great distances, and varying terrains and climates.

"If we could fly here, we could fly anywhere, and such has proved to be the case."

A pictorial history

Top: The School of Aerial Photography stand with their planes and supporting equipment in late 1918. **Bottom:** An aerial camera is installed on a Curtiss JN-4 "Jenny" plane on a side mount in an undated Langley photo. *Air Combat Command History Office photos*
Opposite page: Awaiting their final OK to roll out, 1st. Lt. Cris "2 Shot" Jordan in the front seat and Capt. Matt Guertin ready for an adversary flight against Langley F-22s on Aug. 21, 2015, the day that Langley's 71st Fighter Squadron officially was reactivated. It was designated as the 71st Fighter Training Squadron, and 17 T-38 aircraft provides realistic adversaries for the 1st Fighter Wing F-22 training missions. *Daily Press file photo*

Top: Five F-15 Eagles return to Langley after a month-long deployment to South Korea. In a 1978 file photo, Capt. and Mrs. John Baker, foreground, and Capt. and Mrs. Clay Jones celebrate their reunion. **Bottom:** Langley's first F/A-22 Raptor arrives in May 2005 with pilot Lt. Col. Jim Hecker, 27th Fighter Squadron commander, at the controls. **Bottom:** Vapor trails off the wingtips of an F-22 Raptor during a flight demonstration of its capabilities at Langley Air Force Base in 2014. *Daily Press file photos*

Top: Members of the Fife and Drum Corps from Colonial Williamsburg march in front of a static display of an F-15 as they rehearse for the Air Combat Command's Tattoo at Langley Air Force Base in 1995. **Bottom:** President Barack Obama arrives at Langley Air Force Base in Hampton and meets with military personnel in 2013. *Daily Press file photos*

Top: This photo from 1930 shows construction progress on the NCO quarters at Langley. *Air Combat Command History Office photo* **Bottom:** F-22 Raptors sit at Langley Air Force base in Hampton in April 2012. *Daily Press file photo* **Opposite page:** The 1938 movie "Test Pilot," starring, from left, Spencer Tracy, Myrna Loy and Clark Gable, was filmed mostly in California, but a few scenes were shot in Hampton in December 1937 with Langley enlisted men as extras. When the movie debut in July 1938, billboards on the Peninsula promoted the movie's local ties to Langley. *U.S. Air Combat Command History Office photo*

Top: A photo from April 1943 shows a variety of bomb sizes. *U.S. Air Combat Command History Office photo* **Bottom:** A French Nieuport plane is shown in 1917 with Capt. J.C. Bartolf, left, and Lt. E. LeMaitre. *Library of Congress photo*

Top: The lighter-than-air hangar at Langley Field in 1925. *Air Combat Command History Office photo* **Bottom:** A Boeing Y1B-17 flyby near the Italian liner "Rex," about 800 miles east of New York City is pictured. *U.S. Air Force photo*

Top: A volley and flyby of the 1st Tactical Fighter Wing of Langley Air Force Base were part of a ceremony in 1981 honoring the nation's war dead at Hampton National Cemetery. **Bottom:** Langley Air Force Base is covered in snow in December 1958. **Opposite page, top:** During the Air Power Over Hampton Roads air show in 2006, a heritage flight of U.S. Air Force aircraft features, clockwise from top, F-86 Sabre, F-15 Eagle, A-10 Thunderbolt II and F/A-22 Raptor. **Opposite page, bottom:** A T-38 jet takes to the air at Langley Air Force Base on Aug. 21, 2015, after Langley's 71st Fighter Squadron officially was reactivated. *Daily Press file photos*

The trolly trooper ride was popular at Kid's Day at Langley Air Force Base in 1969. *Daily Press file photo*

CPSIA information can be obtained at www.ICGtesting.com
Printed in the USA
BVOW08s0930290816

460124BV00001B/2/P